FIRST SCIENCE

Gravity

by Kay Manolis

Consultant:
Duane Quam, M.S. Physics
Chair, Minnesota State
Academic Science Standards
Writing Committee

BELLWETHER MEDIA · MINNEAPOLIS, MN

Note to Librarians, Teachers, and Parents:

Blastoff! Readers are carefully developed by literacy experts and combine standards-based content with developmentally appropriate text.

Level 1 provides the most support through repetition of high-frequency words, light text, predictable sentence patterns, and strong visual support.

Level 2 offers early readers a bit more challenge through varied simple sentences, increased text load, and less repetition of high-frequency words.

Level 3 advances early-fluent readers toward fluency through increased text and concept load, less reliance on visuals, longer sentences, and more literary language.

Level 4 builds reading stamina by providing more text per page, increased use of punctuation, greater variation in sentence patterns, and increasingly challenging vocabulary.

Level 5 encourages children to move from "learning to read" to "reading to learn" by providing even more text, varied writing styles, and less familiar topics.

Whichever book is right for your reader, Blastoff! Readers are the perfect books to build confidence and encourage a love of reading that will last a lifetime!

This edition first published in 2009 by Bellwether Media.

No part of this publication may be reproduced in whole or in part without written permission of the publisher. For information regarding permission, write to Bellwether Media Inc., Attention: Permissions Department, Post Office Box 19349, Minneapolis, MN 55419.

Library of Congress Cataloging-in-Publication Data
Manolis, Kay.
  Gravity / by Kay Manolis.
    p. cm. – (Blastoff! readers. First science)
  Includes bibliographical references and index.
  Summary: "Simple text and full color photographs introduce beginning readers to gravity. Developed by literacy experts for students in kindergarten through third grade"–Provided by publisher.
  ISBN-13: 978-1-60014-226-0 (hardcover : alk. paper)
  ISBN-10: 1-60014-226-5 (hardcover : alk. paper)
  1. Gravity–Juvenile literature. 2. Matter–Properties–Juvenile literature. I. Title.

QC178.M366 2009
531'.14–dc22   2008021303

Contents

What Is Gravity?

A basketball player jumps high off the ground. What happens next? He comes back down to Earth. That's gravity at work.

Gravity is a natural **force**. Earth's gravity
pulls everything and everybody toward Earth.

You can see examples of Earth's gravity all around you. Gravity pulls a rollercoaster down a track and a skier down a mountain.

You can see gravity at work in nature. It pulls raindrops down to Earth. It makes water rush over waterfalls.

fun fact
Sir Isaac Newton was the first person to describe gravity. He lived in the 1600s.

It even keeps the moon moving in its **orbit** around Earth. Without Earth's gravity, the moon would drift off into outer space!

Everything Has Gravity

Earth is not the only object that has gravity. In fact, every person and object in the universe has its own gravity. That means everything has a force that pulls on other objects. The gravity of most objects is much too weak to be noticed.

Even this bat and this ball pull on each other with their own gravity.

fun fact

When you get into bed at night you could be just a little bit shorter than when you got up in the morning. This is because gravity pulls on your body as you stand up all day.

The strength of gravity depends on an object's **mass**. Mass is the amount of **matter** in an object. Earth has enormous mass.

Only the gravity of objects with enormous mass, such as planets and stars, is strong enough to be noticed.

The sun has more mass than 300,000 Earths. The sun's gravity is powerful enough to pull on all the planets in the **solar system**. This keeps the planets moving in their orbits around the sun rather than flying out into space.

! fun fact

Gravity helps you balance. Your ears have tiny parts that hold a liquid. Gravity pulls on this liquid. This pull helps you to tell up from down. If these parts in your ears did not work correctly, you would get very dizzy.

The moon's gravity pulls on Earth. The moon's mass is less than Earth's, so its gravity is weaker than Earth's. Even so, the moon's gravity is strong enough to affect our planet.

The moon's gravity causes the water in the oceans to rise and fall twice each day. These changes in ocean water levels are called the **tides**.

Measuring Earth's Gravity

Weight is a measure of the force of Earth's gravity on the mass of an object or a living thing. Earth's gravity pulls harder on objects with a lot of mass. This barbell has a lot of mass. The weightlifter must push very hard against gravity to lift the barbell.

These beach balls are filled with air. They have far less mass than the barbell. The force of Earth's gravity on them is much weaker. These girls can easily lift the beach balls.

Earth's gravity gets weaker when you get farther from the center of the planet. If you stood on a tall mountain, you would weigh a tiny bit less than you would at the bottom.

What if you took a spaceship to the moon? Earth's gravity would pull slightly less as you traveled away from the planet. But don't worry. Earth's powerful gravity would be strong enough to help pull your spaceship home again.

Glossary

force—a push or pull; force can cause an object to start, stop, or change the direction of its movement.

mass—the amount of matter that an object contains

matter—anything that has mass and takes up space; everything on Earth is made of matter, even air.

orbit—the path of a smaller body around a larger body, such as a satellite around a planet, or the earth around the sun

solar system—the sun and the many bodies that move in orbit around it; our solar system has eight planets and their moons, an asteroid belt, and many comets.

tides—the rise and fall of ocean water each day; tides are caused by the moon's gravity pulling on the oceans.

weight—a measure of the force of Earth's gravity on a living thing or object

To Learn More

AT THE LIBRARY

Bradley, Kimberly Brubaker. *Forces Make Things Move*. New York: HarperCollins, 2005.

Hewitt, Sally. *Amazing Forces and Movement*. New York: Crabtree, 2008.

Mason, Adrienne. *Move It! Motion, Forces, and You*. Toronto, Ont.: Kids Can Press, 2005.

ON THE WEB
Learning more about gravity is as easy as 1, 2, 3.

1. Go to www.factsurfer.com

2. Enter "gravity" into search box.

3. Click the "Surf" button and you will see a list of related web sites.

With factsurfer.com, finding more information is just a click away.

Index

The images in this book are reproduced through the courtesy of: hans.slegers, front cover; NBAE / Getty Images, pp. 4-5; Daniel Berehulak / Getty Images, p. 6; All Canada Photos Inc., p. 7; Kevin Tavares, pp. 8-9; Todd Taulman, pp. 10-11; VINCENT GIORDANO, pp. 12-13; Jurgen Ziewe, pp. 14-15; YASAR, p. 16; Andy Williams / Getty Images, p. 17; Stuart Franklin / Getty Images, p. 18; Elena Elisseeva, p. 19; Brad Wrobleski / Masterfile, pp. 20-21.